Together Again

I Talk You Talk Press

Copyright © 2018 I Talk You Talk Press

ISBN: 978-4-907056-75-9

www.italkyoutalk.com

info@italkyoutalk.com

All rights reserved. No part of this publication may be resold, reproduced, stored in retrieval system, copied in any form or by any means, electronic, mechanical, photocopying, recording or otherwise transmitted without the prior written permission from the publisher. You must not circulate this publication in any format, online or otherwise.

This is a work of fiction. Names, characters, businesses, organizations, products, places, events and incidents are either the products of the author's imagination or are used in a fictitious manner. We have no affiliation with any existing companies mentioned in this story. Any resemblance to actual persons, living or dead, existing stories or actual events is purely coincidental.

Although the author and publisher have made every effort to ensure that the contents of this book were correct at press time, the author and publisher do not assume and hereby disclaim any liability to any party for any loss, damage, or disruption caused by errors or omissions, whether such errors or omissions result from negligence, accident, or any other cause.

For more information, see the Copyright Notice on our website.

Image copyright: © lkunl - Fotolia.com #75830425 Standard License
© Kirsty Pargeter - Fotolia.com #41652896 Standard License

CONTENTS

1. Facebook	1
2. Jacques Villemont	3
3. The great surprise	6
4. Arrival in Tokyo	9
5. Akina's apartment	13
6. Akina explains	16
7. Questions, questions, questions	19
8. A plan for the day	22
9. A day out in Tokyo	25
10. Okonomiyaki and photographs	27
11. A phone call	30
12. Yokohama	32
13. Prisoners	36

14. Nick's story	38
15. Breakout	41
16. Disaster	45
17. Do they believe us?	47
18. A better day	49
19. What next?	53
Thank You	56
About the Author	58

1. FACEBOOK

Chrysa Melias walked onto the balcony of her parents' house. She looked down at the Aegean Sea far below. It was a beautiful day, and she was free to do anything. She could call her family's driver and tell him to take her into town, or she could drive herself. She could call a friend and meet for lunch, go shopping, have a manicure, or go to a movie.

I don't want to do any of those things, she thought. *I'm very lucky. I have everything I need. I have no money worries. I can have an easy and luxurious life. But I am bored. If I didn't have the Internet, I would go crazy.*

She went to her room and turned on her computer. She signed into Facebook and went to a private group page called 'The Holiday Club'. It had only six members. After their adventure and wonderful vacation in France in the summer, Jarmo had set the page up for them all.

My friends here in Greece are boring, Chrysa said to herself. *They are only interested in fashion and parties, and getting married. I wish I were with my new friends. I wish I were with Pachai, Jarmo, Hehu, Shelley and Akina. I wish we were on a bus somewhere, with no money, and some kind of crazy plan.*

There was a new message from Hehu. He had posted a picture of himself with a cow.

---"Farmers don't have pets, but this cow is special. I call her Brieuc. I gave up my university studies when I had to come back here to help run the farm. I thought I didn't need to study European languages anymore. But after our time in France, I changed my mind. I have applied for a distance learning course, and I am going to finish my degree."---

Chrysa added a comment.

---*"Good for you! Tell me what you are going to study! Maybe I can learn the same language and we can practice together."*---

She read through the other news. Shelley was going back to Australia.

---*"It is very far from most of you, but my Mum has been ill. I think I need to spend some time with her. And I miss the sun!"*---

Akina had added a comment to Shelley's message.

---*"Come to Tokyo on your way back to Australia!"*---

Chrysa smiled. When she first met her, Chrysa thought Akina was very sweet and cute and shy. But Akina was a very surprising and strong person. She had a job with an international company in Tokyo. She was doing very well in her career.

Not like me, thought Chrysa. *I don't do anything.*

There was a new post from Jarmo too. He had posted a map of the world with Helsinki in the middle. Underneath he had written,

---*"Anywhere you want to go in the world, you have to travel through Helsinki!"*---

There were no new messages from Pachai. Chrysa was worried about him. A month ago, Jarmo's mother had died in Helsinki. Pachai and Chrysa met in Paris and travelled together to Finland to support Jarmo, and to go to the funeral. On the way back Pachai had told Chrysa about his problem. His family wanted him to marry soon. His mother was choosing a wife for him. "I will marry the woman my mother chooses," he told Chrysa. "But not yet. I have told my family that I will be a better doctor and a better husband if I have more experience of life. My uncle has lived in Paris for many years. He understands, but my family in India cannot understand."

Chrysa understood Pachai's problem very well. "My family wants me to marry the son of a family in our town," she said to Pachai. "It would be a good marriage. But I don't want it. Not now. I have known Michalis all my life. He is like a child, and he is very spoilt."

"Chrysa! Chrysa!" Chrysa's mother was calling her. "Come down here. Michalis has come to visit you."

2. JACQUES VILLEMONT

While Chrysa was talking to Michalis, a doctor was standing next to a hospital bed in St Brieuc in France. The man in the bed was very old. He had recovered from a bad head injury two months before, but then later, he had got sick. This time, it was cancer.

"I'm very sorry M. Villemont," said the doctor. "The results of the tests are not good. It is bad news."

"Am I going to die?" asked the old man.

"Well, yes," said the doctor.

"How long do I have to live?"

"Maybe three weeks," answered the doctor. The doctor was unhappy. He liked M. Villemont.

The old man reached out and touched the doctor's hand.

"I know it was hard for you to tell me. But it's OK. I'm tired. It's time for me to die. I will see my wife again, and I will see my nephew who died twenty years ago."

The doctor went away and Jacques Villemont lay in his bed and thought about the things he wanted to do before he died. He rang the bell next to his bed. A nurse came running.

"M. Villemont. What is wrong? Can I help you?" she asked.

"Yes," said Jacques. "I want you to call the police station. I want you to find the policemen who came to my house two months ago. Some young people came into my house by mistake, and then a poor man with mental problems tried to kill them. The police will remember. Find the policemen who came to my house that night, and ask one of them to come and see me."

The nurse thought it was very strange, but she telephoned the police station. After a while, she was able to talk to one of the policemen who had talked to the young foreigners.

"M. Villemont is dying," she said. "He wants to talk to you as soon as possible. Could you come?"

The policeman was puzzled, but he said, "I'll come to the hospital in the afternoon." Jacques talked to the policeman for a long time. The policeman was listening carefully. The nurse was worried that M. Villemont was getting too tired, but then the policeman stood up. "It is very unusual, but I think I can help you."

The next day a messenger delivered a letter from the police to M. Villemont.

"Do you want me to read it to you?" asked the nurse.

"No. It's not necessary, but thank you," answered Jacques. "Please call my lawyer. The name and telephone number are in the notebook in that drawer. Please tell him to visit me."

When the lawyer came, Jacques said he wanted to make a will. He said, "When I die, I want the young people to have my money." The lawyer was shocked.

"M. Villemont! You only met these young people once. Why do you want to give them your money? There must be better people to give your money to!"

"I have no family," said Jacques.

"Well then, give your money to the hospital or the church!" said the lawyer.

Jacques was silent for a while. He closed his eyes and remembered. He remembered the day the young people had come to see him in the hospital. Six strong, attractive, young people. The handsome young Indian who was going to be a doctor. The tall New Zealander with the quiet voice and beautiful eyes. He was a farmer, but he talked to Jacques about rugby. The short blond man from Finland. And the young women. The short one with the red hair reminded him of his wife. She had the same energy and happy smile. The tiny Japanese woman who was so gentle and shy. Jacques smiled to himself. *I thought she was delicate, and then they told me she was a karate black belt!* And the beautiful blonde woman.

The lawyer coughed.

Has M. Villemont gone to sleep? he asked himself.

Jacques opened his eyes.

"I will try to explain," he said. "They are six young people from different places. Maybe some of them come from rich families, but I think mostly they have to earn money for themselves. And they came here, to this hospital, to see me. It was like the United Nations. They seemed strong, and they were doing things with their lives. Also, I thought they were having fun! There was not much fun in my life when I was young. I wanted to do things. I wanted to travel and to study, but there was no money, and also, I was afraid. So I stayed here. I married a local woman. We were happy, but she died. Then, there was my nephew Pierre. He was strong. He had great plans, but he was killed in a car accident. I want to give those young people the chance. If they have a little extra money, maybe they can do more. The information is all in this letter. The police gave it to me. So listen to me! I will not change my mind!"

3. THE GREAT SURPRISE

About a month after the lawyer visited Jacques Villemont in the hospital, the old man died. It was a very small funeral. The lawyer was at the funeral, and he was surprised to see a policeman there. He talked to the policeman. They talked about the strange will of Jacques Villemont.

The next day, the lawyer called his secretary into his office and gave her a letter.

"Make six copies of this letter, and I will sign them," he said. "We will mail them this afternoon."

A week later, Jarmo Virtanen came home from a weekend away. He picked up his mail from the box in the front entrance of the apartment block where he lived. He looked at one of the letters. *That's strange,* he thought. *Who is writing to me from France?*

He opened the letter and read it as he was climbing the stairs. He stopped suddenly, and read the letter again. Then he ran up the rest of the stairs. He unlocked his apartment door and threw his bag on the floor. He turned on his computer and opened the Facebook page called 'The Holiday Club'.

Seventeen thousand kilometres away, a man stopped a farm bike by a mailbox. He took out the letters. One of them was from France. He put the other letters in the box on the back of the bike. He opened the letter from France, and read it. Then he read it again. He folded the letter and put it in the pocket of his overalls. He started the farm bike and rode across the fields to the milking sheds. He opened the gates, and the cows came in to be milked. As he worked, he smiled.

Well, Shelley believes in miracles and magic, he said to himself. *Maybe she's right.*

Over the next two days, the six members of the Holiday Club emailed and messaged each other many times. Jarmo was trying to organize a group video call. With so many time zones and such busy people, it wasn't easy. But finally he found a time when everyone could join in.

When they were all on-line together, everyone was talking and laughing at once. Then Jarmo said, "Quiet everyone! We need to make a plan."

"Before we make any plans," said Shelley, "I want to make sure I understand. The old man that we found in the house in Brittany died, and left us some money."

"Yes," said Jarmo. "The money is in the bank, and every year for three years, the lawyer will send us all a small amount of money."

"Did he die because of that head injury? The one he got from falling over in the wine cellar?"

"No," said Chrysa. "I called the lawyer to ask about M. Villemont's family. I thought we must not take M. Villemont's money if there were family members who didn't get anything. But the lawyer told me he had no family. The lawyer said he recovered very well from the head injury, but then, just two months later, the doctors at the hospital found he had cancer."

"OK," said Shelley. "But why did he want to give us his money? When he had his accident, we helped him, but we didn't do anything special. It was just a lucky chance."

"It wasn't because of that," said Pachai. "I talked to the lawyer too. Remember we went to see M. Villemont in the hospital? Well, he liked us. He told the lawyer we were young and travelling and having fun. He wanted to do that when he was young, but he never got the chance. So he decided to give us his money. He wanted us to do all the things he couldn't do when he was young. His house will be sold and the money from the house is going to Nils and his mother. You know, his nephew's friend. The guy who thought we had killed M. Villemont."

"That was a sad story," said Hehu. "I'm pleased he did that."

"So am I," said Akina.

"The bank will give us the money for three years. But there is a rule," said Pachai.

"What's the rule?" asked Shelley.

"That we use the money to travel and do things together. There will be enough money, maybe, for two trips a year if we are careful," said Pachai.

"What happens after the three years?" asked Jarmo.

"I don't know," answered Pachai. "The lawyer said that M. Villemont didn't want us to know."

"So anyway," said Shelley. "It's magic. We can get together again. Where shall we go, and when can we go?"

Everyone talked at once, but in the end it was agreed that the best time for everyone was in July.

"OK. Two or three weeks in July," said Jarmo cheerfully.

"Wait a minute everyone," said Hehu. "Akina. You're not saying anything. When is a good time for you?"

"Uh, everyone. I'm so sorry. But I only started my job six weeks ago. In Japan, it is very difficult to ask for a vacation when you have only been working for a short time. I won't be able to join you."

Everyone was quiet. Then Shelley started to laugh. "We don't know where we want to go! But this makes it easy! Why don't we go to Japan to see Akina?"

"I like that idea," said Hehu. "Chrysa, Pachai, Jarmo. How about you? Would you like to go to Japan?"

"I've never been to Asia," said Chrysa. "I would love to go to Japan!"

"Me too," said Jarmo. "Pachai? Is Japan good for you?"

"Of course," said Pachai. "Akina, would it be OK? Can you help us to find places to stay and things to do?"

"Oh, yes!" Akina was excited. "You can go to Kyoto, you can stay in a Buddhist temple, and you can meet my family! Yes! Please come!"

4. ARRIVAL IN TOKYO

Everyone booked their own air travel. They found very cheap flights. Jarmo took a flight from Helsinki to Moscow, and then from Moscow to Tokyo. Chrysa met Pachai in Paris, and they took a direct flight to Tokyo. Hehu took a flight to Sydney and stayed for a few days with Shelley and her mother. Shelley's mother was feeling much better. Then he and Shelley took a flight to Korea, and another to Tokyo. Everyone was arriving at different times. So they made a plan. Shelley and Hehu were arriving last, so everyone planned to go to the arrivals hall to meet them. Akina was coming to the airport too.

--- *"I am so excited."*--- Akina posted on Facebook. ---*"We will all be together again! I can't wait!"*---

When Pachai and Chrysa walked into the arrivals hall of Terminal 1 at Narita Airport, Jarmo was waiting for them.

"Hi!" he called out. Chrysa ran to Jarmo and hugged him. Pachai and Jarmo shook hands. "How was your flight?" asked Jarmo.

"OK," answered Pachai. "How about yours?"

"We left late from Moscow, so I have only just arrived."

Chrysa was looking at her phone and frowning. "I have to change the time. What time is it here in Japan? When will Shelley and Hehu arrive?"

"It's ten thirty am," said Jarmo. "Shelley and Hehu's plane will arrive at one pm. So we have to wait."

"Let's find somewhere to eat," said Pachai. "I hate airline food and I'm very hungry!"

They found a casual restaurant on the first floor. Pachai and

Jarmo ordered noodles.

"I plan to try a lot of different Japanese food while I'm here," said Jarmo.

"Me too," said Pachai.

Chrysa laughed. "You two think about eating all the time! I am going to have coffee, but nothing to eat."

The noodles were called soba and they tasted very good.

"Next time, I'll try the noodles called udon," said Jarmo.

After they ate, they sat in the arrivals hall and relaxed.

"What time will Akina arrive?" asked Chrysa.

"She will come before Hehu and Shelley's flight arrives," said Pachai. "We should watch out for her. I am sure she will be early."

"Let's walk around and see if we can find her," said Jarmo.

Chrysa sat with their luggage. Pachai and Jarmo walked around the arrivals area. There were many Japanese people in the terminal, but they did not see Akina. Finally, they heard the announcement for the arrival of Shelley and Hehu's flight. They walked back to Chrysa and took their bags. Then the three friends walked to the big doors to wait for Hehu and Shelley.

"There they are!" shouted Pachai. "They are coming now!"

"Where?" Jarmo and Chrysa couldn't see them. Then Chrysa saw Shelley's red hair. Shelley was jumping up and down, and waving. Behind her, was her cousin Hehu. He was smiling.

Shelley pushed through the crowd and reached Chrysa, Pachai and Jarmo. Hehu was close behind her. They all hugged and Shelley said, "Together again! It's wonderful!" Then she stopped and looked around. "But where's Akina? I thought she would come to the airport."

"We thought so too," said Chrysa. "We looked for her, but we didn't see her."

Then Hehu spoke. "I don't know where Akina is. But look there." He pointed to a young Japanese woman standing about 20 meters away. She was holding a large sign. Printed on the sign were their names.

---*Chrysa, Shelley, Hehu, Pachai, Jarmo – Welcome to Japan.*---

They hurried over to talk to her.

"Hi," said Pachai. "Did you come to meet us?"

"Yes," said the young woman. "I am Mie Kobayashi. I am Akina's friend. She couldn't come to the airport. She asked me to come to meet you."

"Thank you," said Chrysa. "That was nice of you. I'm Chrysa. I come from Greece."

Mie smiled. "I know," she said. "I have seen many photographs of you."

She turned to Shelley. "I know that your name is Shelley. You are Australian, but you live in London."

"It's nice to meet you, Mie," said Shelley. "Yes. You are right. I am Shelley. I lived in London for a while, but now I am back in Australia. Do you know which one of these guys is my cousin, Hehu?"

Mie waved her hand at each of the young men. "Hehu from New Zealand, Jarmo from Finland and Pachai from India, who lives in Paris. Is that right?"

Everyone laughed.

"Perfect!" said Pachai. "We are all pleased to meet you. But where is Akina? Is she busy at work?

"No," answered Mie.

"Is Akina ill?" asked Shelley?

"No," answered Mie slowly. "I don't think so. I will take you to her apartment. My English is not so good. I can't explain well. But Akina will tell you. Please come with me."

"Just a minute," said Pachai. "I don't have any Japanese money. Can we please go to a money exchange?"

"Of course," said Mie. "I forgot. Akina told me about that. I have never been outside Japan, so it is hard for me to remember. There is a money exchange over there."

Everyone picked up their backpacks and followed Mie to the money exchange. When they all had some yen, they walked to the airport train station.

Mie stopped at the ticket machines.

"We will take three different trains," she said. "First we will take the Keisei Skyliner to Nippori Station. Then we will change to the JR Yamanote line, and finally we will change at Ikebukuro Station for a train to Kawagoe. It is in Saitama Prefecture. That is where Akina and I live."

"Is the Skyliner a shinkansen? A bullet train?" asked Jarmo. "I am looking forward to traveling on a bullet train."

"No," said Mie. "But it is a very fast train." Mie showed them how to buy their tickets. It was very easy.

Everyone enjoyed the train trip to Kawagoe. They enjoyed looking out of the window. The scenery was different from the scenery in their countries. Chrysa was sitting next to Mie, but Mie was very quiet. She didn't speak at all. Chrysa thought Mie was shy.

"You speak English very well," she said to Mie.

"Thank you," said Mie. "But my English is not as good as Akina's. I am sorry. I should tell you about the sights we can see out the window. But I am so worried about Akina."

"What is wrong with Akina?" asked Chrysa.

Mie shook her head. "Akina will tell you," she said. "I am pleased you came to Tokyo. I must return to my hometown tonight. My brother is getting married. I didn't want to leave Akina alone. It is good you are here. Please look after her."

5. AKINA'S APARTMENT

When they arrived at Kawagoe Station, they walked for about 15 minutes until they came to a very narrow street between tall buildings. Mie stopped and looked around the street. It was empty. Then she pointed to a tall old apartment building.

"Akina's apartment is on the sixth floor," said Mie. "My apartment is on the eighth floor. We are very lucky we can live in the same building."

Why don't they share an apartment? thought Shelley. *Why do they pay for two apartments?*

They tried to get into the small elevator, but it was too small for six people with backpacks and hand luggage.

"I'll walk up," said Jarmo.

"So will I," said Hehu. "I was sitting for so long on the plane, and on the train. Did you say the sixth floor?"

"Yes, that's right," said Mie.

Jarmo and Hehu left their backpacks in the elevator and walked up the stairs. When they reached the sixth floor, Shelley, Pachai and Chrysa were standing next to the elevator door with the luggage. There were two apartment doors. Mie was standing next to one of them. She was talking to Akina through an opening in the door.

"Akina doesn't want to open the door," said Chrysa. "I am very worried."

"Akina, it's OK," said Mie. "Your friends are all here. It is safe. I didn't see anyone else in the street. Open the door."

The door opened a little, and they could see Akina's face. The chain was still on the door. She looked around carefully. Then she unhooked the chain and opened the door wide. "Quickly!" she said. "Come in quickly!"

"Akina," said Mie. "I have to go now. You will be OK. Your friends will help you."

Mie turned to the others. "I have to leave now. It was nice to meet you. Maybe I will see you again."

Mie ran to the stairs. They could hear her hurrying up towards her own apartment.

"Quickly," said Akina.

They carried their backpacks and hand luggage into Akina's apartment. It was very small. It was only one room with a kitchen at one end. The bathroom was near the door. The room was hot and dark. The windows were closed, and the curtains were closed too. It was very crowded with six people and their bags. Shelley looked around the apartment.

This is an apartment for only one person, she thought. *I guess Mie's apartment is just as small.*

Chrysa hugged Akina. "It's wonderful to see you!"

"Are you OK?" asked Shelley. "What is the problem?"

"Yes, Akina. You must tell us. What is the problem?" said Jarmo.

Akina sat down on a sofa against the wall. She looked up at all of them.

"It is wonderful to see you. I feel better now that you are here. I am so frightened."

"What are you frightened of?" asked Pachai.

"Japan is a very safe place," said Jarmo loudly. "Why are you frightened?"

"Stop everyone," said Hehu. "We all want to listen to Akina, but let's do it slowly and quietly."

He walked over to curtains and opened them.

"Don't!" cried Akina.

Hehu turned around. He spoke softly to Akina. "It's OK. We are here, and nothing bad will happen to you."

Outside the tall windows was a small balcony. Hehu opened the windows and carried the backpacks outside. He put them down on the balcony.

"Now we have enough space to sit down and talk."

"Hehu is right," said Jarmo. "I'm sorry I spoke loudly to you. It is because we are all so worried."

"I know," said Akina. "It's OK. I understand. But it is so hard to explain."

"Shall I make some tea?" asked Chrysa.

"Yes," said Akina.

"I'll help you," said Shelley. "It will be my first chance to do something in a Japanese kitchen."

Chrysa filled the kettle with water and put it on the gas burner. Shelly looked for cups. In the cupboard she found five beautiful new cups. They were all different. Each one had a nametag tied to the handle. There was one for each of them and on the nametags, Akina had written, "Welcome to Japan!"

"What is wrong?" Shelley whispered to Chrysa. "Three days ago on Facebook, Akina was so happy and excited. Now she looks terrible!"

"I don't know," Chrysa whispered back.

They made tea and poured it into the beautiful new cups. They carried the drinks back into the main part of the room. Akina was sitting between Hehu and Pachai on the sofa. Hehu was holding her hand. Jarmo was sitting on the floor opposite the sofa. Shelley and Chrysa handed out the tea. Everyone liked their cups very much. Shelley and Chrysa sat down on the floor next to Jarmo and waited.

6. AKINA EXPLAINS

Akina drank her tea thirstily. Then she started speaking.

"You know I work for an international company in Tokyo. It is an import-export company. The company buys things from other countries and sells them to Japanese department stores and supermarket chains. It also sells Japanese products to other countries.

"I am new, so my job is quite simple. I check the orders. Especially, I check the English and Japanese on the orders to make sure the information is the same. If it is not the same, I sometimes have to call companies in other countries to check, or maybe call someone in Japan. I like it. I can use my English a lot and I talk to interesting people. Everything was good until a few days ago. The trouble started on Tuesday night.

"My boss is American and he is very nice. I asked my boss if I could have a free day today because I wanted to go to the airport to meet you. He said that was OK, but I had to finish checking this month's orders first. So on Tuesday I worked late, so that I could finish checking this month. I worked until around eleven pm.

"There was no one else in the main office, the door was closed, and it was quiet, so I finished everything. Then I thought I heard someone in one of the small offices down the hall. I heard the elevator door open and close twice. I thought I could hear a cart or trolley too, but I didn't think about it. I wanted to go home. I packed up my work and left the main office. When I was waiting for the elevator, the door to one of the small offices opened and closed. The elevator arrived and I got into it.

"I was walking to the station when I heard someone behind me breathing hard. I work near Shinjuku Station, so there were many people on the streets even at eleven thirty at night. So I wasn't worried. I just thought it was someone hurrying to catch a train. And then…"

Akina stopped talking.

"It's OK, Akina," said Pachai. "It's OK. Take your time."

"Would you like another cup of tea?" asked Chrysa.

"No, no," answered Akina. "I'm OK. But it sounds so crazy. I was standing at the side of the road waiting for the traffic lights to change so I could cross. There were people all around. Suddenly, someone pushed me hard, and I fell forward onto the road. A taxi just missed me. Some kind people helped me stand up. I was OK, but I felt shaky.

"Then on the down escalator in the railway station someone pushed me hard again. I held onto the rail and I didn't fall. I looked behind me, but there were just normal looking people. On the train platform at Shinjuku nothing strange happened, and when I changed trains at Ikebukuro, the platform was almost empty.

"But when I got off the train at Kawagoe and walked home I thought someone was following me. I couldn't see anyone. It was just a feeling. I walked very fast because I felt nervous. I got in the elevator, and then it stopped between the fourth and fifth floors. The lights in the elevator went out for a while. Then the lights came back on. I called Mie on my smartphone. She ran down the stairs to the first floor to wake up the building manager. But the elevator suddenly started again. When she got to this floor, I was getting out of the elevator. But Mie saw someone on the stairs. A man was coming up the stairs. When he saw Mie, he turned and ran down the stairs again."

"Poor Akina," said Shelley. "What a terrible night. I understand why you feel so nervous!"

"No!" said Akina. "I wasn't nervous then. I thought it was strange, but I wasn't nervous."

"So what happened the next day?" asked Jarmo. "Did you go to work?"

"Of course," said Akina. "I didn't have any bad feelings at all. Mie and I walked to the train station together. She works near Ikebukuro. She has a job in an insurance company. When I got to Shinjuku, I bought a lunchbox from the convenience store near my office. I often do that if I get up late and have no time to make my lunch.

"I put my name on the lunchbox and put it in the refrigerator in the main office. At lunchtime I went to get my lunchbox, but I could not find it. I guessed the reason. There is a man who works in the storeroom. He is very lazy, and he is not a nice person. He spends all his money on gambling. Sometimes he steals other people's lunchboxes. No one sees him do it. So no one says anything. But everyone knows about it.

"That afternoon, something terrible happened. The man from the storeroom became very ill. They called an ambulance and took him to the hospital. But he died. No one knows why he died. The hospital laboratory is doing tests. But the boss told me that the doctors at the hospital thought he died from poison!

"When I left work I thought someone was following me again, but I never saw anyone. I stopped at the supermarket near the station and bought some sandwiches. I didn't have lunch, so I was very hungry. When I arrived back here, I ate the sandwiches. I felt very tired and I lay down and went to sleep. I woke up when Mie rang the doorbell. She had to ring it many times before I heard it. My room was full of gas. There was a hole in the gas pipe. If Mie had not come to see me, I would have died.

"I stayed the rest of the night with Mie. The next morning I came back here. The building manager called the gas company and they fixed the gas pipe. Then I called work and said I was sick. I am too frightened to go out. I am sure someone is following me. I am sure someone wants to kill me!"

7. QUESTIONS, QUESTIONS, QUESTIONS

"We need another cup of tea," said Shelley. She stood up and went back to the kitchen. Shelley was very shocked by Akina's story. She thought Akina was in real danger.

"Akina," said Chrysa. "Why didn't you stay in Mie's apartment? It would have been safer."

"Mie is my friend. I stayed with her that night. But maybe if I stayed there every night, she would be in danger too."

"Did you tell the police?" asked Pachai.

"Mie and I talked about it. I am not sure Mie believes me. She thinks maybe all the things that happened were a coincidence. She thinks maybe I am very tired from working too hard, and it has made me very nervous. Mie said the police will say the same thing. I am sure she is right."

Shelley came back with the teapot and poured more tea for everyone.

"What about your family? Have you talked to your family?" she asked.

Akina shook her head. "No. My family would say, 'Come home. Working in Tokyo is too hard for you.'"

Hehu had been listening to everyone. Now he spoke.

"Questions, questions, questions. We are all very tired from traveling. We are hungry too. We need to eat and relax. We need to sleep. Tomorrow, we can make a plan. But I have one question. Where are we going to stay tonight?"

Akina smiled. "I hope my plan is OK. I have the key to Mie's apartment. She has put three futons on the floor. They are for Pachai, Jarmo and Hehu. It will be crowded, but I hope you will be comfortable. Shelley, Chrysa and I will sleep here."

"Sounds great," said Jarmo. "Now, why don't we eat?"

Akina jumped up from the sofa. She looked much happier. "I have a refrigerator full of food! I planned to cook for you!"

"No, no," said Pachai. "Not tonight. You are tired."

"You can help me cook," said Akina.

"No. Not tonight," said Pachai again. "Where can we buy takeaways?"

"There is a hamburger shop about one block away," said Akina. "The hamburgers are good. They have kebabs and vegetable croquettes too."

"Let's go," said Jarmo. Akina explained how to get to the hamburger shop. Jarmo and Pachai went out. Akina gave Mie's apartment key to Hehu and he took Jarmo's, Pachai's and his own backpack upstairs and put them in the apartment. Hehu took a shower and dressed in clean clothes. Then he walked downstairs to the 6th floor, and stood with his back against the wall watching the elevator and the stairs. Jarmo and Pachai soon came back with bags of food.

"We bought food from a convenience store for breakfast too," said Pachai. "And don't worry about not eating Japanese food! We bought a pack of sushi."

"And the hamburgers are made with Kobe beef!" said Jarmo, laughing.

Akina felt better as they put the food out on the low table in the middle of the room and sat on the floor around it. Everyone was hungry, and they laughed and joked as they ate. When the meal was over, they cleaned up and said good night. They were all tired.

Jarmo, Pachai and Hehu went upstairs. Jarmo had bought beer, and they sat on their futons, drinking beer and talking.

"Do you believe Akina?" Jarmo asked Pachai.

"Yes, I believe her. I don't know if everything is connected, or what it means, but I think everything happened."

"So you are not sure, but you didn't want us to eat anything out of Akina's refrigerator, did you?" Jarmo smiled at Pachai.

"No. But maybe these events are connected. Maybe the man who stole Akina's lunchbox died of poison. If he died of poison, the person who poisoned the food in the lunchbox could also poison the food in Akina's refrigerator. I thought it was better to be very careful, but I didn't want to frighten Akina. But someone got into her apartment and put a hole in the gas pipe. So maybe they could poison the food in her refrigerator too."

"Did someone put a hole in the gas pipe? Or was the hole in the gas pipe an accident?" asked Jarmo.

Hehu took another bottle of beer.

"You know these things happened to Akina. Her instinct tells her she is in danger. I think the events are all connected. I don't know why, but someone is trying to kill her. We have to trust her feelings. Remember what she did in St Brieuc?"

"I will never forget!" laughed Jarmo. "The man was going to kill Shelley and Chrysa. We couldn't do anything. Then Akina saw what was happening. She climbed out of an upstairs window and down a stone wall. She walked quietly across the garden and attacked the gunman. It was amazing."

"I'm puzzled," said Pachai. "Akina is so strong and so brave. Why is she so frightened and nervous now?"

"I think it's easy to understand," said Hehu. "Many people are like Akina. They are very brave and very strong about things they can see and understand. The problem for Akina is that she can't see where the danger is coming from. She will be very active when she knows what the danger is, and when she can see it. It is very difficult for her, because she knows that most people will not believe her story."

Hehu picked up the empty beer bottles and took them to the kitchen.

"I think the girls will be safe tonight. We can make a plan in the morning," he said.

"I've been thinking about that," said Jarmo. "I have some ideas already."

"Good," said Pachai. "I am so tired I can't think. I'll have a shower and sleep. Then tomorrow maybe I can help you with the plan."

8. A PLAN FOR THE DAY

Hehu woke up early. Pachai and Jarmo were still sleeping. He dressed and left Mie's apartment. He walked down to the 6th floor and stopped at the door of Akina's apartment. He listened. It was very quiet. He walked down to the street and across to the other side. He looked up at the balcony of Akina's apartment. There was no one in the street and he couldn't see anything strange. He bought coffees from a convenience store and walked back to the apartment building.

Pachai and Jarmo were awake and waiting for him when he walked into Mie's apartment.

"Coffee! Wonderful!" said Pachai. "Thank you! It seems that Mie doesn't drink coffee. We couldn't find any."

"I went down to Akina's apartment and listened at the door," said Hehu. "There was no sound. I think the girls are still sleeping. But we must think about a plan for today."

As they drank their coffee, Jarmo talked about his plan. Pachai had some ideas too.

"I think it will work," said Jarmo. "What do you think, Hehu?"

"I think it is a very good plan, but we must ask the others about it. Akina will have to be very brave because she is the target. But I think she will agree."

"Yes. I know it is a risk," said Pachai. "But Akina must do this. It is important to know who wants to hurt her."

Hehu stood up and stretched.

"The enemy you can see is better than the enemy you can't see. When you know the enemy, you can plan an attack."

Jarmo laughed. "You know, Hehu. You are so quiet, but sometimes I think you are very scary!"

"Good," said Hehu. "I hope whoever is trying to kill Akina thinks so too!"

Jarmo's smartphone rang. It was Chrysa.

"We're all awake and hungry. What are we eating for breakfast?"

"I hope you didn't eat anything from the refrigerator!" Jarmo was worried.

"No, no. I understood Pachai's warning. It's OK. I explained to Akina. I took everything out of the refrigerator. And then I took many things out of the cupboards. I threw everything away. But now we want breakfast!"

"Sure," said Jarmo. "We bought a lot of breakfast food yesterday. We will bring some to Akina's apartment."

"Good," said Chrysa. "I will make coffee."

While Chrysa, Shelley and Akina were eating breakfast, Jarmo explained his plan.

"Is it OK for you, Akina?" asked Shelley. "It will be frightening for you. But we will all be there, and we will take care of you."

Akina took a deep breath. She looked worried but she said, "Yes. I will do it. I have to know who is following me, and why."

Hehu was looking down at the street. He could see two men in the street. One man was standing across the street. He was reading a newspaper. There was another man standing on the corner. He had blond hair. He was drinking coffee and looking at Akina's apartment building.

They might be normal people or they might be the people who are trying to hurt Akina, thought Hehu. *I don't know.*

He turned to look at the others. "I think there might be more than one person," he said quietly. "But maybe we can find out today."

"Now Chrysa, Shelley, Akina," said Jarmo. "Here is the map. This is the route you will follow today. We have copies of the same map. We will always be close to you."

"We must be sure that no one in the street sees Pachai, Jarmo and I leave this building," said Hehu. "Is there another way out?"

Akina told them about a back door to the apartment building.

"Jarmo and I have some things to arrange," said Pachai. "We should go now."

Pachai and Jarmo left Akina's apartment by the back entrance.

The others drank more coffee and studied the map. Then Hehu left. He went out the back door and across an area with garbage bins. He climbed the fence at the back of the area and found a narrow road. He walked to the next street and then to the railway station.

Akina, Shelley and Chrysa dressed for a day out shopping and sightseeing. They walked out to the main road. Akina was quiet and nervous. She wore a big hat and sunglasses. She walked between Chrysa and Shelley. She looked around all the time. At the railway station, they bought tickets for Ikebukuro.

"It will take about thirty minutes to get there," said Akina. "Then we will change to the Tokyo Metro to get to Ginza."

"Ginza!" said Chrysa. "It will be wonderful. I can't wait to see all the shops! I must buy something very nice for my mother while we are there."

On the train, Akina chose a seat next to the window. Chrysa sat next to her.

"Are you OK?" she asked Akina. "I know this is very hard for you."

"I'm OK. But I am worried that you are all in danger too."

"We'll be fine," said Chrysa. "We are all together again. We can look after each other. But Akina, you can't walk around all day in that big hat and sunglasses. If someone is following you, they must be able to see you!"

Akina took a deep breath. "I know," she said. She took off the hat and sunglasses and put them in her bag.

9. A DAY OUT IN TOKYO

The three young women had a busy day. They went to Ginza, a famous shopping area. Then they went to the Imperial Palace Gardens and walked through the park area. It was Saturday, so there were many people enjoying the open space in the middle of the busy city.

In the afternoon, they visited the Sannomaru-Shozokan, the Museum of the Imperial Collections, and enjoyed looking at the kimonos and paintings, and went to the National Museum of Modern Art.

Everywhere they went, a tall man followed them. Sometimes, he was more than 10 metres behind them, but whenever they crossed a busy street, he came up very close. He was always there. He also visited the same museums as the young women.

In the morning, Chrysa, Shelley and Akina took the same route as a young man in a suit. They followed him through Ginza and along the streets to the Imperial Palace. He seemed to be interested in people, because he took many photographs of the streets. It seemed to be a popular day for sightseeing by bicycle too. There was always a man on a bicycle near them. In the morning, it was a blond man wearing brightly coloured shorts and a baseball cap. After lunch, it was a dark haired man in jeans. These men liked taking photographs too. They took photographs of everything.

Finally, Chrysa, Shelley and Akina went back to Akina's apartment. They stopped at a supermarket and bought food. Akina was very cheerful.

"Today was OK," she said. "I don't feel so nervous now and I want to teach you how to make okonomiyaki! Usually we eat them in restaurants but we can make them at home too."

"Uh. What are we going to cook?" asked Shelley.

"Okonomiyaki. They are like pancakes, or maybe like pizza. You can have different flavours. They will be good for all of us. You and Pachai don't eat meat or fish but you can have vegetables and tofu in your okonomiyaki."

10. OKONOMIYAKI AND PHOTOGRAPHS

Back in the apartment, they unpacked their shopping. Akina opened her empty refrigerator and sighed.

"I filled the refrigerator with all kinds of exciting and interesting food for you to try. Now it's all gone!"

"I know, Akina. It was terrible to throw everything away, but if the man from your office was poisoned, we couldn't take the chance," said Chrysa.

"You are right. We must be careful." Akina looked very worried and upset.

Shelley hugged her. "It's a pity," she said. "But we have food for tonight. So teach us! I want to learn how to make something Japanese."

Hehu arrived about ten minutes later. He had climbed the fence behind the apartment building and come in through the back door. Then Pachai arrived. It was almost an hour before Jarmo came in. He was laughing.

"Sorry I'm late! I had to take the bicycle back to the rental cycle place. Then when I arrived here, an old woman saw me climbing over the fence behind this building. She started shouting at me. I ran away and waited until she had gone."

"Dinner is almost ready," said Akina. "We have prepared everything, but you have to cook your own."

"What?" said Jarmo. "Pachai and I have been taking turns to ride that bicycle all day. We have walked and walked. Then I was chased by that old woman! I am too tired to cook!"

"If you don't cook your own okonomiyaki, you won't eat," said Shelley, laughing.

"OK," said Jarmo. "But do I have time for a shower?"

"Hurry," said Chrysa.

By the time Jarmo came back from Mie's apartment, everyone was sitting on the floor around a low table. There were bowls of pancake mixture mixed with cabbage and many other interesting ingredients. Akina had put small gas burners on the table and everyone made their own okonomiyaki.

The meal was a great success.

"Heaven," said Pachai. "If all Japanese food is like this, I'm staying here."

"You might have to stay here." Shelley said, laughing. "You ate so much, you probably can't move."

"Now, to work," said Jarmo. "I will load all the photographs we took today onto my iPad and we can look at them."

Everyone else tidied the living area and washed the dishes.

Then they sat on the floor and looked at the iPad. Jarmo had loaded the photographs in time order and made a slide show. At first everyone was talking and laughing, but as they watched the slide show, the room became very quiet.

Finally Hehu spoke. "There are two men," he said. "Can you start the slide show again, Jarmo?"

Jarmo reloaded the slide show.

"Pause it now," said Hehu. He leaned forward and pointed to the screen. There was a man with blond hair in the picture.

"This man in the picture, the man with the blond hair. I saw him before. He was out on the street in front of this apartment when we were having breakfast. And here he is on the street in Ginza."

Jarmo went through the pictures slowly. They could see the blond man in many of the pictures. Sometimes he was walking next to Hehu.

"Do you know this man, Akina?" asked Pachai.

"I think I have seen him somewhere, but I am not sure. I don't know who he is."

A different man had followed Akina, Chrysa and Shelley in the afternoon. Akina was sure she had never seen him before.

"So what do we know?" asked Shelley.

"There were two men following you three girls when you were out today. The photographs show them clearly," said Jarmo. "Can we show the photographs to the police?"

"I'm not sure," answered Pachai. "What would the police say about us taking photographs? And will they believe Hehu? He saw two men in the street outside the apartment this morning. One of them, the one with blond hair, followed Akina this morning. But maybe the police will not believe him.

"The problem is, we have photographs of the men who are following Akina. We know they have been trying to kill her. But we don't know who they are, or why they are doing this."

"Akina?" asked Hehu. "Are you sure you don't know these men?"

"Yes, I'm sure. One of them I may have seen somewhere. But I don't know their names or anything about them."

"OK," said Hehu. "Then tomorrow we will follow them!"

"No! It will be too dangerous," said Chrysa.

Akina agreed with Chrysa. "They will see you. You are foreigners. You will be easy to see."

"We'll think about it," said Hehu.

11. A PHONE CALL

The next morning, they ate breakfast together in Akina's apartment.

Pachai, Jarmo and Hehu wanted to find the mystery men and follow them. But Chrysa, Shelley and Akina would not agree. They thought it was too dangerous.

While everyone was talking, Hehu was standing at the window. He was looking down onto the street.

"I don't think we need to worry about what to do," he said. "There is no one in the street. Maybe the men don't work on Sundays."

Just then, Akina's phone started to ring. She looked at her phone.

"Nick is calling me. He's my boss at work," she said. "Why is he calling me on a Sunday? Shall I answer it?"

"Why not?" said Shelley. "You said your boss is very nice. Maybe he has some news about the man who died."

Akina answered the call. Everyone watched her as she listened to the voice on the other end of the phone. Then she said, "I'm sorry, Nick. I don't know. Can I call you back please?"

Akina looked at her friends. "Nick says he has something very important to talk about with me. He wants me to go and meet him at his apartment. I said I will call him back. What do you think? Shall I go?"

Five people spoke at once. "Yes!" "No…"

"What does he want to talk to you about?" asked Chrysa.

"He didn't say," answered Akina. "He just said it was very

important and urgent."

"Akina must find out what is happening," said Jarmo. "I think maybe Nick knows something."

"But why didn't he tell Akina on the phone?" said Shelley. "I don't like it. I think it might be dangerous."

They talked about it for a few minutes. Then Pachai said, "Listen. It is not a good idea for Akina to go to Nick's apartment alone. But if Akina says she will meet him in a public place, like a restaurant, it will be safer. And, of course, we will all go."

"Maybe he will say 'no'," said Chrysa.

"If he wants to help Akina, he will say 'yes'. If he says 'no', then maybe he is the bad guy," said Pachai.

Akina called Nick. "Can you talk to me about this very important thing on the phone? No? OK. Well I will come to Yokohama to meet you. But I don't want to go to your apartment. Is there a restaurant near there? I will write the address down. My friends arrived on Friday, so they will come to Yokohama too."

Akina finished the telephone call. "He says he would like to meet you. We will meet him for lunch in a restaurant near his building," she said. "I wanted to take you to Yokohama. This will be a chance for you to do some sightseeing. It will take about an hour and a half to get to Yokohama from here. And then we have to go to the restaurant, so we should leave here by ten o'clock."

"Great," said Jarmo. "I want to see Yokohama, but the most important thing is to solve this problem and to keep you safe."

"Do you think it matters if anyone sees us together?" asked Chrysa.

"No," said Hehu. "It doesn't matter."

Akina got a little nervous when they were out on the street. But with her friends around her, she soon felt better. Everyone enjoyed the train trip to Yokohama. They relaxed and talked to each other. No one talked about Akina's problem or the meeting with Nick.

12. YOKOHAMA

Nick lived in an old warehouse near the port.

"He is very lucky," said Akina. "The company owns the building. There is a storage area downstairs that is used by the company. Upstairs, there is an apartment. Nick lives there."

The building where Nick lived was old and traditional, but some of the nearby buildings had been renovated. There were shops and restaurants on the ground floors of the buildings. They met Nick in a restaurant opposite his apartment.

"I am very pleased to meet you all," said Nick, shaking hands with everyone. "Akina has been so excited. She has been planning your vacation for weeks."

Nick knew the people in the restaurant well. He asked the waiter to put two tables together near the window so that they could all sit together.

"Let's have a drink before we order," said Nick. "Who wants tea and who wants coffee?"

Nick went to the counter of the restaurant and paid for drinks for everyone. After the teas and coffees arrived, Akina said, "What do you want to talk to me about? Is there a problem? Why couldn't you tell me on the phone?"

"I think there is something wrong," said Nick. "You called to say you were sick. But I didn't think that was true. We heard from the family of the man who died. The doctors at the hospital told them he died from poison. I think you know something about this. I think you are frightened of the police. I want to help you. So I want you to tell me everything you know."

Akina didn't say anything. There was another table very close to them. Two men were sitting there drinking beer.

"I don't think we should talk about these things here," she said. "Someone might hear us."

Nick laughed. "We're talking in English! No one here will understand what we say."

"OK," said Akina. "Please understand. I am not frightened of the police. But I think someone is trying to hurt me or kill me."

"Why?" Nick laughed again. "Why would anyone want to hurt you? You are an office worker. You are imagining things."

"If you don't think Akina is in danger, why did you ask her to come here?" asked Chrysa. "I think you know something about what is happening. So why don't you tell us?"

"No. I don't know anything. But I am worried about Akina. She must tell me everything she knows."

Akina looked at her friends. Their faces told her that they were not happy.

What shall I do? she thought. *My friends are worried. They don't want me to talk. But Nick is my boss. He is always nice to me. I will have to tell him.*

Akina told Nick everything. She told him about working late and hearing people in the office in Shinjuku late at night. She told him about being followed. She told him about being pushed onto the road and pushed on the escalator. She told him about the elevator stopping, and the man on the stairs. Then she said, "The next day, my lunchbox disappeared from the refrigerator in the office. I think the man from the storeroom stole my lunchbox. He ate the food, and then he died. Do you know anything about that, Nick?" she asked.

"His family thinks it was an accident," said Nick. "They think he ate something bad. But the police came to the office to ask questions. You weren't there. So maybe they will come and talk to you later."

"That's good," said Akina. "I want to talk to them."

"You want to talk to them about being pushed on the escalator, and the problem with the elevator in your apartment?" asked Nick, laughing. "They will think you are crazy."

"Maybe they will. But I don't mind. In the beginning, I thought I was having a bad day, but it was nothing special. Then other things happened."

"What happened?" asked Nick.

"The next thing was the gas leak." Akina explained about the gas leak.

Nick looked worried, but he said, "Akina, you had a bad time. So many bad things happened, but it doesn't mean anything. Just a lot of bad things happened to you over a couple of days."

"What about the lunchbox?" asked Shelley. "It was Akina's lunchbox that was missing. The man from the storeroom stole it. Then he was poisoned and he died. Maybe someone wanted to kill Akina."

"Yes, maybe Akina's lunchbox had something bad in it," said Nick. "Maybe the lunchbox shop was not careful. But it could still be an accident."

"Or someone could have taken the lunchbox from the refrigerator. Akina's name was on it. They could have put poison in her food!" Shelley was angry.

"But who?" asked Nick. "We don't have people like that working in our company! I believe that Akina had some bad luck, but I don't think she has to worry about the police. We can forget about it. Akina, come back to work after your vacation with your friends. We will never talk about this again."

"We don't think the things that happened were bad luck," said Pachai. "We think something very bad is happening."

"We didn't think anyone would believe Akina's story," said Jarmo. "So we decided to get some evidence. Yesterday, Akina, Shelley and Chrysa went shopping and sightseeing. Hehu followed them all day. Pachai and I were there too. We looked like tourists. We hired a bicycle and we took photographs of everyone who came near Akina."

He took his iPad from his backpack, and put it on the table.

"Look at these photographs."

He showed Nick the photographs of the two men.

"This man with the blond hair, and this other man, followed Akina all day. Now do you believe her?"

"It seems very strange. Maybe there is something wrong," said Nick. "But I don't think the police will believe you."

"Do you know these men?" asked Pachai.

"No! Of course not!" said Nick. "Do you think I know men like that?"

While everyone was talking, Hehu was looking out of the window.

"I think you do know these men," said Hehu. His voice was very cold. "The man with the blond hair has just walked into the building where you live."

"But there's a storage area downstairs," said Nick. "It has nothing to do with me."

"It belongs to the company, doesn't it?" said Chrysa. "And now I understand why Akina thought she had seen the blond-haired man before. You have dark hair, but your faces are alike. Who is the blond-haired man? Your brother? Your cousin?"

13. PRISONERS

Suddenly the men at the next table stood up. One of them stood behind Jarmo and the other stood behind Shelley.

"Uh," said Jarmo very quietly. "This man behind me has a knife."

"No!" said Nick. "You said they would be safe! You said you wouldn't do anything!"

"Just stand up and walk out of the restaurant," said the man standing behind Shelley. "I have a knife against her back. I will kill her if you don't do what I say."

"Walk slowly and normally," said the other man. "Walk across the street and into the building across the road. We are following you. If you try to do anything, both your friends will die!"

Everyone stood up and slowly left the restaurant. They walked across the street. The two men followed closely. Hehu looked back at them.

Maybe I can do something, he thought.

One of the men had one arm around Shelley's waist. He was holding a knife in his other hand. He was pushing it against her chest. The other man had his arm around Jarmo's neck. He was smiling, but Hehu could see he was holding a knife across Jarmo's neck.

Too dangerous, thought Hehu. *I can't do anything now. I will have to wait.*

A door in the building across the road opened.

"Go in," said the man holding Shelley. "Go in, or your little friend will die."

Akina, Pachai, Chrysa, Hehu and Nick walked into the storage area. The two men pushed Jarmo and Shelley in behind them. The door closed. It was very dark. They couldn't see anything.

Then they heard the click of a switch and the room was suddenly filled with light. The blond-haired man was standing at the end of the room. He had a gun.

"You said you wouldn't hurt them!" shouted Nick. "You promised!"

The blond-haired man laughed. "They know too much. We can't let them go. They will talk to the police."

Hehu turned around to look at the two men from the restaurant. They were still holding Jarmo and Shelley. Jarmo looked at Hehu. The knife against his throat had cut him a little. Hehu could see some blood running down Jarmo's neck. Jarmo did not look frightened. He looked very, very angry, but he shook his head.

Jarmo is right, thought Hehu. *Not now. We have to wait.*

"Put them in the back room," said the blond-haired man. "We have some work to do before we can move them to the boat."

He pointed his gun at them while the other two men pushed Jarmo and Shelley through a door at the back of the room.

"Now all of you go in there," he said to the others. He pointed his gun at Nick. "You too, little brother!"

As they walked into the back room, the men took everyone's phones and backpacks. Then the door was closed and they heard the sound of a heavy key in the lock. Next, they heard the sound of bolts sliding across the door. Pachai ran to the door and tried to open it. He pushed it. He tried to break it down with his shoulder. It was impossible.

He turned around to look at the others. The room had no furniture. Shelley was sitting on the floor. Akina was hugging her. Akina was crying. Chrysa had taken a tissue from her pocket. She was trying to stop the blood from the cut in Jarmo's neck. Nick was sitting on the floor with his face in his hands.

Hehu was standing in the corner of the room. He was looking at the wall. There were no windows, but high on the wall there was a small opening. It was closed with iron bars.

"Can we get out through that opening?" asked Pachai.

"Maybe," said Hehu. "But we can't get those iron bars out without making a lot of noise. I think we should wait."

"While we are waiting," said Chrysa, "Maybe Nick can tell us why we are here."

14. NICK'S STORY

Everyone looked at Nick.

"Yes," said Akina. "I trusted you. I told you everything, and now my friends are in danger. Tell us why."

Nick took his hands away from his face. He started to talk.

"I have lived in Japan for eighteen years. I love it here. I like my job. My brother is older than me. He is a criminal, but he is lucky. The police never caught him. But life was becoming dangerous for him in the USA. So he came to visit me here. He was very interested in my apartment. It is so convenient. It is near the port, and it has this storage area downstairs. He met some Japanese gangsters, and they started a business.

"They brought guns into Japan. It is very difficult to get guns here. They are very expensive, and, of course, they are not legal.

"My brother and his friends paid men on foreign fishing boats to bring the guns to Japan. They kept the guns in this room."

"But, why did you let your brother do it?" asked Chrysa. "Did he pay you money?"

"No, no," said Nick. "I didn't want him to do it. I asked him to go away. I told him I would tell the police."

"Why didn't you tell the police?" asked Pachai.

"I am frightened of my brother. He said he would kill me."

"Did you believe him?" asked Pachai.

"I don't know. He is a very bad person. Maybe he would not kill me, but his friends are very dangerous. I am scared of them. I am sure they would kill me."

"That is very bad," said Jarmo. "But what happened? Why did your brother and his friends start following Akina?"

Nick looked at Akina. "I'm sorry, Akina. I really like you. I never wanted anything bad to happen to you. But this is what happened.

"They hid the guns here under my apartment. They waited until they found someone who would pay a lot of money for one of the guns. But of course they never let the buyers come here to Yokohama. They met the buyers in Tokyo. Sometimes they met the buyers at the company's offices in Shinjuku. I never saw them. I gave my brother keys to the offices. They met the buyers there late at night. My brother told me they would meet a very important client, who wanted many guns, at the office on Tuesday. I told him the offices would be empty. I didn't know Akina was going to work so late. Even people who work late in our company go home about seven thirty, or eight pm.

"They met their client in one of the small offices. The door to the main office was closed. They didn't know anyone was there until they heard the elevator. They saw Akina get into the elevator. They didn't know how long she had been there. They didn't know if she had seen them, or seen their client. Their client was very angry. He said, 'You must kill her.' I am so sorry, Akina. It was bad luck that you were there."

"OK," said Jarmo. "I understand what happened on Tuesday night. But what about Wednesday? How did they poison the food in Akina's lunchbox?"

Nick looked very sad. "That was me," he said slowly. "They tried to attack Akina on Tuesday night. But they were not successful. So my brother came back to my apartment. He told me that maybe Akina had seen something at the office. It was important that she didn't talk to anyone. He never told me that the men wanted to kill Akina. He gave me some drug. He told me to put it in Akina's tea at work. He said it would make her a little sick and a little sleepy. That's all. He said Akina would want to go home. He said that was all they needed. If Akina didn't talk to anyone for twenty-four hours, they would be able to finish the deal. Then they would close down everything here in Yokohama and move to another city in Japan.

"I believed him. I didn't want to hurt Akina, I thought if she was at home sick, she would be safe. I wanted my brother to go away. So I said I would do it.

"When I got to work, I had a good idea. I put the drug in some food in Akina's lunchbox. But that guy from the storeroom stole Akina's lunch, and ate it. Then he died! It was a nightmare! I understood then that my brother and the other men wanted to kill Akina. But there was one good thing. I knew you were staying with Akina. I knew she was not alone. I thought maybe she would be safe."

"I don't understand," said Pachai

"What don't you understand?" asked Nick.

"You knew your brother and his friends wanted to kill Akina. So why did you ask to meet us today?"

"My brother wanted to know if Akina had seen anything on Tuesday night. He wanted to know if she had told you anything. He said if you didn't know anything, all of you would be safe. I wanted to help Akina. I thought my brother and his partners would just go away and forget about her."

"So the men in the restaurant were there to listen!" said Shelley.

"Yes. My brother didn't trust me. He said they would be listening to every word."

"It was very difficult for you," said Akina softly.

"No!" said Nick loudly. "Don't be nice to me. You are all in terrible danger, and it is my fault. I knew my brother was selling guns, but I didn't stop him. I helped him because I was frightened. I was very weak."

"What are they going to do with us?" asked Chrysa.

"I think they will take us all out on a boat. I think they will kill us. They will throw our bodies into the sea. They will disappear to another part of Japan or maybe even another country."

"So your own brother will kill you?" asked Chrysa. She was very shocked.

"Maybe yes, maybe no," answered Nick. "But it makes no difference. If he doesn't kill me, one of the others will. He will not try to save me.

"Maybe I don't care. I killed the man who stole Akina's lunch box. If he hadn't stolen the lunch box, I would have killed Akina. I didn't know it was poison. I added it to the food, but it is still my fault. But I don't want any of you to die!"

Nick started to cry.

15. BREAKOUT

Pachai was still standing near the door. He put his ear against the door.

"I can't hear any noise out there. Do you think they have gone?"

"That door's thick," said Jarmo. "Maybe they are still there. What time is it?"

Chrysa was the only one with a watch. "It's a little after two o'clock," she said.

"Nick," said Pachai. "You said they would take us to a boat. What time do you think they will do that?"

"Maybe not until after dark," said Nick. "They will want to wait until it is dark so no one will see us. We will be locked in here until night time."

"I don't think so," said Hehu. "We will escape before then."

"How?" asked Nick.

"I don't know," said Hehu. "But we will think of something. First, we must take the metal bars out of that opening. But we must be quiet. Akina, if I lift you up to the opening, can you look and see how the bars are attached?" asked Hehu.

"OK," answered Akina.

Hehu put his hands out and Akina stepped onto them. Then he lifted her up onto his shoulders.

"It's dark in here and it's hard to see", said Akina. "But there are two pieces of wood with holes in them. The metal bars go through the holes. The wood is old. Maybe we can break the wood."

"OK. I'll lift you down now," said Hehu.

When Akina was back on the ground, Hehu said. "We need a tool. Even if the wood is old, we can't break it with our fingers."

"How about my hair clip?" asked Chrysa.

Everyone looked at Chrysa. Her long blonde hair was folded up in a bun. She had a metal hair accessory to hold the bun in place. Chrysa took the clip out of her hair. She gave it to Hehu. It was silver with tiny blue flowers. It was very pretty.

"It doesn't look very strong," said Hehu. "But we can try. Jarmo, how is your throat? Does it hurt?"

"A little," answered Jarmo. "But the cut is not deep. I'm fine. If I am not too heavy for you, I will try to get the bars out."

Jarmo climbed onto Hehu's back and looked at the metal bars. "It's going to take a long time," he said. "Are you OK, Hehu?"

"I'm OK for a while," said Hehu.

"Tell me when you need a rest," answered Jarmo and he started work.

Pachai and Chrysa stood by the door and listened. They could not hear anything. Pachai knelt down and looked at the lock.

"The key is in the lock," he said.

Chrysa laughed. "If we were characters in a children's storybook, we would be able to slide some paper under the door, knock the key out and slide it back in here. Then we could unlock the door!"

Pachai laughed too. "That's true. We could do that if we had some paper. But there are also the bolts! But you have given me an idea."

Pachai took a pen from his pocket. He pushed the pen into the keyhole and pushed the key out. They heard the sound as it fell on the floor outside.

"Now we can see a little," he said. Pachai and Chrysa took turns to look through the keyhole. They couldn't see very much of the room outside but it seemed to be empty. They could not hear any sounds either.

Akina and Shelley sat on the floor and chatted. Akina was teaching Shelley some useful Japanese words.

After about thirty minutes, Jarmo said, "I'm coming down. I have broken almost all the wood around one of the bars, and I think I can pull it out. But I need a rest first. I'm sure Hehu needs a rest too."

After a five-minute rest, Jarmo climbed onto Hehu's back and started working again. "I'm really hungry!" he said. "We didn't eat any lunch!"

"Good," said Hehu. "You are already heavy. I would not want to hold you up if you were heavier!"

The others all laughed. Nick was sitting on the floor in a corner. He felt very bad. When he heard them laughing he looked at them.

I am very frightened, he thought. *I am in a panic. I don't know what to do. But Akina and her friends are so calm. They are not frightened. They joke. They are a team. They make plans and do things. I want to be like them.*

"Aha!" said Jarmo. He waved a metal bar at them. "I got one out. Now it will be quicker. I can use this bar to break the wood around the other bars."

An hour later, all the bars were out of the opening. Jarmo climbed down to the floor. Hehu rubbed his stiff back and shoulders.

They all looked up at the opening in the wall.

"I can get through that space," said Akina.

"So can I," said Shelley. "Akina and I will go through the opening. We will come back into this building and open the door for you."

"No," said Pachai. "I think it is too dangerous. Chrysa and I can't see or hear anything in the room outside, but the men might be in Nick's apartment. They might see or hear you. Go to the police!"

"I agree," said Hehu. "Get away from this building. Find someone with a telephone. Talk to the police."

"OK," said Akina and Shelley. "We'll go now."

Hehu lifted Shelley high in the air. She pushed herself through the opening. The space was very small and it was difficult for her. Finally she managed it. She disappeared and they heard a sound as she landed on the ground outside.

"OK," they heard Shelley call quietly. "I can't see anyone around. Come quickly, Akina."

Akina did not have so much trouble to get through the opening. She was soon outside with Shelley.

"We're going now," called Shelly.

Nick looked at the opening in the wall. There were pieces of broken wood and metal bars on the floor. He was frightened.

"My brother and his partners might come back," he said. "They will be very angry when they see that Akina and Shelley have escaped! They will hurt us!"

Jarmo looked at him. "What is the difference?" he asked. "They are planning to kill us!"

"I hope they come in," said Hehu. "I want to hurt them first."

He picked up the metal bars from the floor. He gave one to everyone in the room. "If they come in here, we might be able to attack them as they come through the door."

16. DISASTER

They waited. No one spoke. Hehu and Jarmo were listening beneath the opening in the wall. Pachai and Chrysa were next to the door. Chrysa was watching through the keyhole. Nick was still sitting in the corner.

Finally Jarmo said, "I think I can hear some people in the street."

"Someone's in the next room," said Chrysa. "Maybe more than one person!"

Hehu moved quickly to the door. He stood on one side with the metal bar in his hand.

"Put it down," said Chrysa. "These people are wearing uniforms!"

They heard the bolts being pulled back. The door opened. There were many policemen.

"Where are they?" asked one of the policemen. "Where are the men who kidnapped you?"

"Maybe they are upstairs in my apartment," answered Nick.

"We will take you out of here," said the policeman.

They walked out of the door and towards the street outside. There were many cars and vans on the street. The policemen held their arms and walked with them towards one of the vans. Akina and Shelley were standing next to the van.

"They're up there," called Shelley. She pointed to the roof of the warehouse. They stopped and looked up. There were policemen with guns on the roof. There were other policemen on the roofs of nearby buildings.

"I can see two men," said Pachai. "Where's the other one?"

Suddenly Nick's brother ran around the corner from a side street. He was holding a rifle. He stopped and aimed it at Akina.

"Noooo!" shouted Nick. He pulled away from the policeman and ran in front of Akina.

Chrysa shut her eyes.

There was the sound of gunshots. Then everything was quiet. Chrysa opened her eyes again. Akina was leaning against the side of the van. She had blood all over the front of her jacket. Nick was lying on the ground at her feet. A few metres away, Nick's brother was lying on the street. A policeman had shot him.

He was dead. But before he died, he had fired one shot. He tried to kill Akina, but he had shot his brother instead.

A policeman was kneeling next to Nick. He said something, and another policeman started talking on his radio.

"Get in. Get in!" said a policeman loudly. He pointed to the van. They all got in and the van drove away.

17. DO THEY BELIEVE US?

The police had found their bags with their passports and money and Jarmo's iPad in the other room of the warehouse. They gave the bags back to them, but they kept the passports, cameras and phones, and the iPad. The police asked for the keys to Akina's and Mie's apartments. They sent a team to search the apartments. When that search had finished, the police finally decided that the six friends could go back to the apartment building. It was almost 1:00am before they were allowed to go. They had been at the police station answering questions and telling their story for eight hours.

An older policeman called Mr Kanayama drove them in a van. Another van followed them.

Mr Kanayama said, "Policemen will stand outside the doors of both apartments all night."

"Why?" asked Jarmo. "Are they protecting us? Or are they there to stop us running away?"

Mr Kanayama looked at him. "Maybe both," he answered. The policemen from the other van got out and ran up the stairs.

They all got into the elevator with Mr Kanayama. At the 6th floor they got out and stood together outside Akina's apartment door. No one spoke. Everyone hugged each other. A policeman unlocked Akina's door, and the three young women went in.

Hehu, Pachai and Jarmo got back in the elevator with two policemen and rode up to the 8th floor.

When they were inside Mie's apartment Jarmo asked, "Do you think the girls will be OK?"

"I'm sure they will be safe," answered Hehu.

"They are all shocked and very tired," said Pachai. "But we know how strong they are. I think they will be OK."

"Let's sleep," said Hehu. "Tomorrow will be a better day."

18. A BETTER DAY

Everyone slept late on Monday morning. After Hehu, Pachai and Jarmo got up and got dressed, Jarmo opened the apartment door. There were two policemen outside. One of them was talking on a mobile phone.

"Can we go down to the other apartment please?" he asked. "We're very hungry, and the food is downstairs."

One of the policemen said, "No. You must stay here."

But then the other policeman finished his phone call and said, "Yes. That's OK. You must be ready to leave for the police station in one hour, so please eat and drink quickly."

The two policemen talked quietly to each other as they walked down the stairs behind Pachai, Hehu and Jarmo. Then they talked to the policemen outside Akina's apartment.

Pachai, Hehu and Jarmo walked into Akina's apartment. Chrysa was putting breakfast food on the low table. Shelley was making coffee. Akina was sitting on the floor near the window. She was very pale. Hehu walked across the room and sat on the floor next to her. He put his arms around her.

"It is almost over," he said. "We have to go to the police station in one hour's time. And then everything will be OK. So just be strong for a little bit longer."

They ate breakfast quickly. Everyone was still very quiet. The memories of the day before were still strong, and they were all still very tired.

Soon a policeman knocked on the door of the apartment.

"The van has come," he said.

When they arrived at the police station they were taken to a big meeting room.

On a side table, they could see their passports, phones, cameras and Jarmo's iPad. The policemen who had been at the apartment building followed them into the room.

"Sit down," said one of the policemen. "Our boss wants to talk to you."

They sat down and waited. Someone brought cups of tea.

Shelley felt very nervous. She looked at the others. Akina was looking at the table. Pachai and Hehu looked very relaxed, but Chrysa and Jarmo looked worried.

What's happening? Shelley asked herself. *I don't like this. It is very strange.*

An older man came into the room. A woman in a smart suit followed him. The man sat at the top of the table and the woman sat behind him.

The man looked at them and smiled.

"I am Matsumoto. I am the senior person at this police station," he said slowly in English. He bowed, and everyone bowed to him.

"I am sorry because I do not speak English well. I will speak in Japanese and Ms Sato will translate into English for you. It is very important that you understand well."

Mr Matsumoto spoke for a long time. Ms Sato translated his words into English.

"You had a very hard time yesterday. We are sorry. You must be very tired. You must think that Japan does not welcome foreigners. That is not true. But you must understand that we must check everything. We spoke to many people at the company. We spoke to Ms Mie Kobayashi. We looked at all the photographs on your cameras and on the iPad.

"Also we arrested some of the gang members. The American is dead, but we have the rest of the gang in prison. They have told us many things about bringing guns into Japan, about the American and his brother, Nick, and about how they tried to kill Ms Akina Tanaka.

"We know that your story is true. Also your photographs will help us. So please enjoy your holiday. We will contact you if we need more information, but I don't think it will be necessary."

Mr Matsumoto bowed. Then he stood up and left the room. Ms

Sato followed him.

A policeman went to the side table and gave everyone their bags and things.

Five minutes later, they were outside the police station. They stood on the street, looking at each other.

Pachai looked at his telephone. "This time on Friday, we were waiting to meet Hehu and Shelley."

Then Pachai started to laugh. After a few seconds Jarmo started laughing too.

Chrysa didn't understand why they were laughing. "What's funny?"

Jarmo and Pachai couldn't speak. Jarmo's face was red. Pachai had tears running down his face. Hehu took control. He put a large hand on Jarmo's shoulder and the other hand on Pachai's shoulder.

"Coffee," he said. "Let's go to a café and drink coffee."

Akina pointed across the road. "There's a coffee shop over there."

They waited for the traffic lights to change, and walked across the road. In the coffee shop Chrysa found a table, and Akina ordered coffee. The coffee came quickly.

Chrysa was still puzzled. "Now, tell me! What is so funny?"

Jarmo drank his coffee very quickly.

"I'm sorry for laughing, everyone. I'm sorry, Akina. But I think Pachai and I had the same thought. We have been in Japan for only seventy-two hours, and it's been like a lifetime of excitement."

Pachai nodded. "We were detectives. We were kidnapped. We were in danger. We spent hours and hours in a police station. We stayed in an apartment with a police guard outside the door. I can't believe it is only three days since I got off the plane at Narita."

Akina looked very worried. "It has been so terrible. I am sure you all want to go home."

"No!" shouted everyone.

The waitress in the café came running to their table. "Is everything OK?"

Akina spoke to her in Japanese. The waitress smiled and went away.

Chrysa laughed. "It is funny. But we did some sightseeing, we saw Yokohama and we ate some great Japanese food. What will we do next?"

Akina opened her bag. She took out an envelope and took out five pieces of paper.

"This was my vacation plan. I made a schedule for every day you are here in Japan."

She handed a schedule to everyone.

Shelley read it. "You didn't plan very much in the first few days. That was lucky."

"No," said Akina. "I thought you would be very tired. So the first two days were just resting and a little sightseeing in Tokyo."

"That's OK then," said Jarmo. "We didn't rest very much, but we did go sightseeing a little. I know we had two gangsters with us, but we did see a lot. So why don't we continue with Akina's plan?"

"What's next?" asked Pachai.

"My plan was to catch a train this afternoon to Gunma Prefecture. My friend Mie's family has a very small traditional onsen high in the mountains. An onsen is like a spa, or hot spring. Then tomorrow I planned to go to Gifu Prefecture. I thought you would like Takayama and Shirakawa-go...."

"OK," said Pachai, laughing. "So let's do it!"

They finished their coffees and walked out of the café. They found the subway station and waited for the train to take them back to Akina's apartment. If they hurried they could pack their bags and be on the train for Minakami in Gunma Prefecture by 3:00pm.

While they were waiting for the train, Chrysa stood next to Akina.

"Akina?" she said. "What did you say to the waitress in the café when we all shouted 'No!' so loudly?"

Akina smiled. She still looked very pale and tired, but Chrysa could see that she was happy.

"I told the waitress that foreigners were a little crazy. I said that I would try harder to keep you quiet!"

19. WHAT NEXT?

Ten days later, they were back in Tokyo. They ate out at a small restaurant near Akina's apartment building. Then they went back to Akina's apartment and drank champagne.

"It has been an amazing holiday!" said Shelley. "Thank you Akina. We had a great time."

"I can't believe we all have to leave tomorrow," said Pachai. "I could stay here for months and there would still be new and interesting things to do."

"I'm sorry there was no time to go to Hokkaido or Kyushu," said Akina. "I wanted you to see as much as possible."

"We saw a lot," laughed Jarmo. "Think of all the things we did."

"Tea ceremony, dressing in kimono, the spa, visiting Akina's family, staying in a temple in Kyoto…" Shelley said.

"The beginning was so bad," said Akina sadly.

Chrysa looked at Hehu. Chrysa and Hehu were worried about Akina. It was a very bad time for Akina. She was very shocked. After everything was finished with the police, Akina tried hard to be cheerful. But sometimes Chrysa and Hehu saw that she was very quiet and unhappy.

Two days before, when they were staying with Akina's family, Akina got some phone calls from Tokyo. After that she talked a lot with her parents. She didn't tell her friends about the phone calls or the conversation with her parents.

"Akina," said Chrysa. "What will happen about your job? Will you go back to the company?"

"No. The owners of the company will send someone new from the USA. They asked me to go back and work for the new manager. But my parents said 'no'. They are very upset and worried. It's OK. I don't want to go back. I have too many bad memories."

"Why don't you come to Greece with me?" asked Chrysa. "My parents would be so happy to meet you, and I would love you to stay with me."

"Thank you Chrysa," said Akina. "But I can't take a holiday now. I want to find a new job. I want to do something different."

"What are you going to do?" asked Pachai.

"I need your advice. Do you remember the woman who translated at the police station for Mr Matsumoto?"

"Sure," said Pachai. "I remember. Ms Sato."

"Yes. Ms Sato. Well she called me when we were at my family home. She told me that she was impressed because I spoke English well. She said that it was great that I had such good friends who were not Japanese. I could work with many different kinds of people. Her brother has a travel company in Canada. He does a lot of business with Japan. She told him about me and he has offered me a job."

"What do your parents think?" asked Chrysa.

"They want me to go. My father says I should leave Japan for a little while. My mother is unhappy that I will go far away, but she agrees with my father."

"So what's the problem?" asked Jarmo.

"Akina," said Hehu. "It is your dream to work in another country for a while. You don't need our advice. Just follow your dream."

"But I don't feel good about myself right now. I am not so confident. I don't know if I can do it."

"Of course you can," said Pachai. "You are one of the strongest people I know. You had a very frightening time and you were so brave. You can do anything!"

"Yes, Akina," said Chrysa. "Do it!"

Akina smiled at her friends. "OK. I will!"

"More champagne!" said Jarmo. He poured more champagne into everyone's glasses. "Stand up and let's drink to Akina's new job and a great new adventure."

"To Akina!" said everyone. They all drank. "We should also drink to M. Villemont," said Pachai. "To M. Villemont!" Everyone drank again.

"Uh, just a minute," said Shelley. "I know we will be communicating on Facebook, but we are all here now so I want to make a suggestion. How do you feel about summer in Australia? How about meeting next time in Sydney?"

"Oh, yes!" said everyone.

"Does everyone still have some champagne in their glasses?" asked Hehu. "Good. Then let's promise to meet in Sydney."

"To Sydney in summer!" they said together. "Cheers!"

I Talk You Talk Press

THANK YOU

Thank you for reading Together Again. (Word count: 15,740) We hope you enjoyed it. The next book in the Holiday Club series is Different Seas.

If you would like to read more graded readers, please visit our website http://www.italkyoutalk.com

Other Level 3 graded readers include
A Dangerous Weekend
A Holiday to Remember
Akiko and Amy Part 1
Akiko and Amy Part 2
Akiko and Amy Part 3
Be My Valentine
Different Seas
Enjoy Your Business Trip
Enjoy Your Homestay
I Need a Friend
Old Jack's Ghost Stories from England (1)
Old Jack's Ghost Stories from England (2)
Old Jack's Ghost Stories from Ireland
Old Jack's Ghost Stories from Japan
Old Jack's Ghost Stories from Scotland
Old Jack's Ghost Stories from Wales
Party Time!

Stories for Christmas
The Curse
Who is Holly?

ABOUT THE AUTHOR

I Talk You Talk Press is a Japan-based publisher of language textbooks, graded readers and language learning/teaching resources.

Our team is made up of highly experienced language teachers and translators, who have all studied at least one additional language to an advanced level.

This experience enables us to design our materials from the perspective of both the teacher and the learner. We consult with both teachers and language learners when designing our textbooks and graded readers, and test our materials extensively in the classroom before publication.

We are a fast-growing press, and currently publish graded readers for learners of English. We publish new graded readers monthly.

www.ingramcontent.com/pod-product-compliance
Lightning Source LLC
Chambersburg PA
CBHW032216040426
42449CB00005B/632